Spartan Leadership

By James DeLuca

Spartan Leadership

Copyright © 2018 Spartan Leadership Group, LLC
www.SpartanLeadershipGroup.com

All rights reserved. This book or any portion thereof may not be reproduced or used in any manner whatsoever without the express written permission of the publisher except for the use of brief quotations in a book review.

Cover and Illustrations by Richard Pace
Edited by David Stahl

All quotations remain the intellectual property of their respective originators. All use of quotations is done under the fair use copyright principal.

ISBN: 9781790527304

Printed in the United States of America

Table of Contents

Introduction 1

Chapter 1: Singular 3

Chapter 2: People Focused 6

Chapter 3: Accountable 10

Chapter 4: Rallying 13

Chapter 5: Trustworthy 16

Chapter 6: Action Biased 19

Chapter 7: Never Surrender 21

Conclusion 23

Introduction

Visionaries with leadership skills achieve extraordinary things. Our history books are replete with the stories of people who dreamed of a better life. They began with an idea or purpose. Like a seed, they planted their idea and nurtured it. By adding the right elements, including labor, their idea eventually came to life. What is the magic word in the last sentence? Labor. For any vision to come to fruition, you must act.

But for an idea large enough to offer something more significant than personal benefit, action alone won't be enough to achieve your objective. People are required, making leadership skill essential to realizing your goal. Leadership skill is your ability to unite people around your vision to deliver it.

The importance of leadership is neither a revelation nor a new concept. But the picture becomes clouded when we attempt to define the "ideal leader." A variety of people come to mind from Adolf Hitler to Mother Teresa. The names I just mentioned are likely not the two you thought of as you read the last sentence. The point is: there is no absolute answer to the question of what makes a great leader. You can be a great leader even if you have one follower.

Your individuality will define your effectiveness as a leader. People who choose to follow you will come in all forms. Others may perceive a person you see as evil as rebellious or revolutionary. A person's willingness to forgive might be viewed as a weakness by some and as a strength by others. The best path to becoming a better leader is *not* by changing yourself to fit a mold.

Improving your ability to lead is about becoming a more authentic version of yourself, then attracting and collaborating with like-minded people to achieve a common goal. This perspective gives you and your organization an incredible advantage – no one is better at being you than you!

When reading stories about visionary leaders, a common theme emerges. They all went through a similar process of personal growth and discovery. Some who grew their organizations ultimately failed as they drifted away from their founding principles. Over the last 3,000 years, there have been many great leaders. This book will focus on one of history's earliest leaders. The Ancient Spartan civilization experienced a significant upheaval around 800 B.C. A rapid transformation of their culture took them from a nation suffering from many societal issues to an icon of invincibility and national pride. One person drove this extraordinary result with a grand vision and the will to execute it. This book is the story of Lycurgus.

Chapter 1: Singular

Many of us have heard of Leonidas, the famous king in Spartan history who bravely fought at the battle of Thermopylae with a band of 300 Spartan soldiers. However, it was a man named Lycurgus who was the father of Spartan culture. Lycurgus was a prince, second in line to take the throne. His father and brother had died; his sister-in-law was pregnant with a child who, if male, would have been the heir to the throne in Sparta. This woman offered Lycurgus the throne, promising to abort the child if he would have her as his queen. Lycurgus feigned support of this plot, warning her not to abort the child, but instead to bring the child to him upon his birth. When the child was born, Lycurgus proclaimed him, Charilaus, as the rightful king of Sparta. The people of Sparta loved Lycurgus for stepping aside in favor of tradition. However, the child's mother harbored hatred for him. To exact a measure of revenge, she wrongly accused him of plotting to murder the child. Seeing the rift ahead, Lycurgus left Sparta for the island of Crete to avoid the feud.

After that, Sparta experienced substantial civil unrest and lawlessness. While planning a return to Sparta after Charilaus grew to adulthood and fathered an heir, Lycurgus traveled the continent observing various forms of government to identify those that would be of most use to Sparta. He focused on resolving the issues that plagued Sparta, identifying many reforms that might help. After years of travel and research, his vision was complete. He traveled to the Oracle at Delphi to receive guidance and insight into how such reforms might affect his civilization. Here he received assurance that his proposed changes would create a better future for the citizens of Sparta.

As a leader, your vision will be your compass for all your decisions. Your ability to correctly identify the strategy to bridge your starting point to your goal will determine your success. Your ability to communicate your vision is the measure of your leadership skill, along with putting people in the right positions to realize that vision. Consider three essential elements as a guide for creating and clarifying your vision:

1. Perceived Benefit - Why would someone want you to succeed, or why would someone help you? Consider:
    a. What's the problem you want to resolve? This challenge is the reason for your existence as a leader.
    b. How will achieving this goal be a benefit to others? By answering this, you have defined the result your organization will strive to accomplish.
2. Skill - What skills are required to complete your mission? Consider:
    a. Skills that you currently possess - this is your foundation.
    b. Skills that you need to develop - skills you need to learn to serve your purpose better.
    c. Skills that are required to support you - skills you need to acquire through partnership.
3. Commitment - Your level of dedication to the mission will be the ceiling for the organization. Consider:

    a.   Is this something you would be willing to commit your time to even if there was no personal gain?
    b.   What are you willing to sacrifice to make this happen?

Your success accomplishing a mission relies on others' perceived benefit of your goal, your critical skills, and your commitment to the task. Looking at Lycurgus as an example, let's review these three vital elements as they pertained to Lycurgus and his mission.

The perceived benefit was high. Most people not only recognized the unrest but were suffering because of it – both commoners and royalty alike. Because of Lycurgus's exemplary leadership skills, the Spartan kings regularly wrote to him, imploring him to return. Such overtures were unheard of in the Spartan culture. Lycurgus's loyalty to Sparta was unquestioned, as evidenced by his choice of justice over personal gain. Furthermore, after leaving his home, he spent his time preparing himself to serve Sparta better, when the time was right.

The first principle of Spartan Leadership is **Singularity**. The purpose of an organization is the epicenter of all its actions. Without a clear goal, an organization will have an inadequate direction and source of inspiration. As a leader, having a singularity of purpose allows for complete clarity in identifying your mission and setting objectives.

Chapter 2: People Focused

After consulting the Oracle, Lycurgus was confident Sparta needed his reforms. Lycurgus gained the support of those closest to him. With all his followers, he finally returned home, ready to implement change. Thinking Lycurgus was returning to claim the throne, Charilaus retreated immediately. Later, he came to understand that Lycurgus's intention was not to take power in Sparta but to reform and serve it.

At that time, two houses ruled Sparta. Inequality and anarchy existed in the system. Charilaus supported the initiative to create a 28-person Senate, to balance power between the two houses, and to give the people of Sparta a voice.

To draw others to your vision, the benefit you wish to achieve must be a high-value proposition. An inspiring idea gains the attention of others, but it is the perceived *benefit* that encourages people to come together. Stating a clear mission and getting buy-in from people are the two primary ingredients in the "leadership" recipe. It's your ability to align people with your vision that will define your leadership legacy.

Lycurgus had to convince two royal houses to reduce their power by adding a check and balance system, namely a Senate. To prompt people to sacrifice something, you must not only be able to offer a more significant benefit, but you must also know the hearts and minds of those with whom you are speaking. In this case, there was a substantial benefit to both houses, but there are four critical elements necessary to gain the commitment of others:

1. Communication – For maximum impact, use the least convenient method of contact. Your actions and your investment of time bring authenticity to your mission.
2. Collaboration – Listen with the intention of understanding the other person's point of view and provide real, actionable resolutions, without judgment. If you want someone to choose to be on your side, you need to display that you're on their side.
3. Realism – Set realistic expectations, particularly with difficult issues. To do this, you must understand all aspects of the situation as well as the ground rules. As a leader, it is not only your responsibility to put people in positions where they can succeed, but also to warn them of any impending dangers.
4. Authenticity – A level of self-awareness and authenticity is necessary for others to buy into your mission. People buy into *who* you are before they buy into *what* you do. Choosing to follow someone you don't trust doesn't typically end well for either party.

Recruiting people to your mission requires communication, not only to those within your organization but to those who benefit from the result. Connection creates demand for the benefit. Consider the above four elements with the people you wish to attract to your mission.

As a leader, you will face continually evolving obstacles in achieving your mission. Overcoming these obstacles requires a dedication to increasing your level of skill. Harry S. Truman was quoted saying "Not all readers are leaders, but all leaders are readers." The idea here is that when you're not using your tools, you should be sharpening them. It is essential as a leader to set aside time and resources for your personal development regularly, so that you may better serve those who put their trust in you.

Part of your limitations as a leader is that you are a single person. If you're the only person growing, you are limiting the capacity of the group. The development of those who follow you is as significant as your personal growth. Developing people requires open, two-way communication to identify their needs and to provide the resources necessary for their personal and professional growth. Discuss your team's development on a regular basis and remain in touch with their obstacles.

When developing yourself and others, there are many ways to receive education, but there is no substitute for experience. When training others, it is imperative that you encourage the application of newly acquired skills and concepts. Not only does this reinforce the training content, but it also creates an opportunity to build the teacher/student relationship. Don't consider a lesson learned until behavior changes to reflect the learning. As a leader, this requires you to allow others to act, while you maintain oversight. Ensuring the success of this part of the improvement cycle is your responsibility as a leader.

The second principle of Spartan Leadership is **People Focused**. People are the essential part of any organization. Without people, there can be no leader, and without a benefit to others, your purpose will not be strong enough to attract supporters. Regularly dedicating resources to the people your organization serves will prevent talent or engagement issues from limiting growth.

Chapter 3: Accountable

Lycurgus believed that the best walls "are not made of bricks, but of men." The Wall of Sparta, known as a phalanx, was made of Spartan soldiers locked together by shield and brotherhood. As you might imagine, this was no simple task. To achieve this, Lycurgus created an educational system called the Agoge that produced soldiers who were both physically and mentally strong. At age 7, boys were removed from their families to train as soldiers in a harsh environment where they learned to be resourceful and self-sufficient. At about age 13, boys selected young adult mentors to guide and teach them to be soldiers. When they were 20 years old, they became eligible to become Spartan citizens and soldiers if their peers unanimously approved them. This system created a new "Spartan Standard" for soldiers.

There were many reasons this system produced excellent soldiers. Younger soldiers were mentored by those who had real experience in battle and understood which nuances were most important to teach. Additionally, mentors modeled the behavior they wanted to instill in their students. Lycurgus himself was a master of martial arts, enabling him to create a system that could produce such warriors.

Providing leadership by example was so crucial to Lycurgus that written laws were forbidden. He believed the principles that would allow the Spartan civilization to thrive were best practiced to develop productive habits by all who led. He considered it more important to do what was right rather than to rely upon written laws. In this way, younger generations would learn these laws by living them, gaining a much more in-depth understanding than if they were only to read them.

As the leader of an organization, every move you make will set the tone for those who follow you. When you receive criticism, are you vulnerable to a fault? When being held accountable, are you sensitive to the other person's perspective? Do you show empathy and understanding when dealing with emotionally-charged issues? Do you serve your organization, or does it serve you? Developing your self-awareness is a vital part of defining your culture through your actions. Failing to conduct yourself in a manner consistent with your stated expectations will result in mixed messaging, causing chaos within your team. Imagine placing importance on punctuality then showing up late to every event. How much value will your team put on being on time to a meeting when their leader arrives 15 minutes late? Your standards are not merely what you say they are: they are equal parts of what you *allow* and what you *display*.

Ultimately, the leader is responsible for the results produced by the team. It is the leader's direction that moves the group toward realizing its vision. "Direction" is the combination of both what you observe and what you communicate. After you have set the tone for conduct within the organization, you can effectively set the tone for reaching goals. After priming your team for productivity, it's important to keep them engaged by regularly assigning new goals. Keep three things in mind when delegating missions:

1. Quantifiable – Where are you starting? How is progress measured? How is success measured? What are the time constraints? Who is responsible/involved?
2. Simplicity – Simplify things whenever possible. Limit as many restrictions as possible. When communicating, focus on the most critical information, not on details of less significance.
3. Meaningful – How does achieving this goal <u>relate to</u> the big picture? When there is accountability to the team and the cause, the perceived importance of the task resonates.

The third principle of Spartan Leadership is **Accountability**. A leader must be able to manage himself before he can effectively lead others. When a leader develops self-awareness and leads by example, he can effectively set the tone for the organization. However, acquiring a skill set requires experience. Drawing upon his experience, a leader provides realistic goals and the direction necessary to achieve those goals. Communicating those goals in a clear and straightforward manner maximizes the opportunity for ownership.

Chapter 4: Rallying

Lycurgus spent the next several years implementing the reforms he had planned. Within a short time, the Spartan culture changed its destiny. Ownership of gold and silver was banned. Quickly, robbery and bribery vanished from Sparta. The land was divided based on merit, rather than the accumulation of wealth, offering better recognition of a person's value to Sparta. Together, all men ate the same food in the public mess halls. Doing so built rapport and removed the desire for one to display wealth or overindulgence. The professions of fortune-telling, prostitution, and trading in luxury items diminished then died. These are just a few examples. Cured of its many cultural and societal "illnesses," Sparta was now unencumbered and began to thrive.

As an organization grows, a leader's sphere of influence needs to expand as well. Let your actions evolve from setting the tone for a small group of people to focusing on the organization's culture, as well as amplifying your message through others. Often, we use the term "Passing the Torch" to signify delegating responsibility to others. Instead of merely passing the torch, use it to light the fires of those around you. Your goal is to give up control, but not responsibility. As the leader, you never give up responsibility; you only gain more responsibility as your team grows.

This change in approach will present a variety of new challenges. Prepare yourself to meet challenges from angles that never existed when everything was directly in front of you. Communication will become more complex, and your role will change. When others begin to take on the responsibility of leadership, the importance of your vision is even more crucial. Without a purpose and a clear vision, actions won't always be consistent across all levels of command. It's the unifying message that allows people to work together in harmony.

You can control everything as the leader of a group, but control changes when you include more leaders. Not everyone will have the same point of view, requiring you to mediate among leaders, or between yourself and another leader. There is no simple formula to guide you since there is an infinite number of situations in which you might find yourself. What I can offer are some best practices that will help you achieve the optimal outcomes in these situations:

1. Speak first to set the tone of the conversation and last to provide direction. In the middle, only ask questions to understand someone's point of view further, not to influence it.
2. When weighing opinions, consider each party's familiarity with the situation and the facts of the matter.
3. When the discussion ends, be sure that all parties support the resolution. Raising all the issues in such talks is essential. Separate meetings after the fact only devalue the communication and create internal chaos.
4. When you disagree with one of your leaders on an initiative, navigate through your position and offer perspective; however, if they persist – commit to empowering that leader.
5. Plan one-way communication; in two-way communication, remain open.
6. Be consistent with the purpose of your company and the vision that everyone has embraced. Doing what

is right is more important than the source of the directive.

In addition to navigating conflicting perspectives, previously used operational methods might become outdated. A leader must be able to set aside his ego to allow change to occur. Such change can come in the form of functional improvement, new technology, or a variety of other innovations. Together, ownership and imagination will result in innovation. We are all born with creativity. Encouraging others to use their imagination will develop it, much the same as exercising to build your muscles. Fostering innovation ensures that new blood is continuously circulating through your organization. Managing change is a critical element in redefining and establishing your organization as a more significant entity.

The fourth principle of Spartan Leadership is **Rallying**. Inspiring others to become leaders dramatically increases the rate at which your organization will grow, but it comes with the risk of less effective communication. By encouraging ownership and imagination, you will drive innovation and evolution. Effective communication will require collaborating across channels regularly. By fostering collaboration and change, you will enable your organization to grow further and evolve.

Chapter 5: Trustworthy

As your team expands and you evolve from a single point of responsibility to many, measure your effectiveness as a leader by your influence. Building trust and security are essential to influencing your team positively.

Trust is a pre-requisite to accountability; it's critical that you can manage yourself before managing others. By maintaining the behaviors that earned the trust of your staff, you provide a living example that will become their guide.

We have established three avenues to build trust.

Sharing information is the first avenue. For a multitude of reasons, maintaining transparency is essential. Being transparent with information allows all members of an organization to be aware of the obstacles confronting the group. Sharing that pain creates a fantastic opportunity- the reward of conquering it collectively! Additionally, when you operate as an open book, your actions come under scrutiny. This scrutiny acts much as the Senate did when the royal families held all the power in Sparta. It is a check and balance system that keeps those in power accountable to the cause. When your actions are honorable and consistent with your purpose, a sense of pride will grow among your team. When there is a sense of pride, people will begin to step up as leaders and hold their peers accountable.

Celebrations are the second avenue to build trust. By recognizing the achievements of others, you reinforce the type of behavior that is worth celebrating. Celebration reaffirms direction, creates memories, and generates excitement within the organization. When holding these events, it's essential to include all relevant members of the organization. For example, if a team has their best sales month in company history, don't celebrate with just the team. Celebrate it with everyone in the building! Accomplishments like this are a team effort (not only your sales team), and it's important to acknowledge that. Your team should feel like they're an essential part of something much larger than themselves.

The third avenue to establish trust is by providing feedback. Feedback usually comes in the form of performance reviews. Having personal, collaborative, and honest discussions where imperfection and vulnerability are on the table incubates trust between leaders and followers. When relevant, being open about your shortcomings is of paramount importance, making it easier for you to elicit honesty and self-awareness from others.

When providing feedback, focus on progress over perfection. Winston Churchill once said: "Perfection is the enemy of progress." When your goal is perfection, you form a habit of failure that will lead to disappointment. By definition, perfection changes by the minute. When your goal is progress, you nurture behavior that results in measuring achievement toward a non-moving target. Easily determine progress by understanding where you started and where you are now.

A feeling of security must accompany trust within your organization, for this allows members to focus on external risks. In each example above, it is the leader's responsibility to provide security. When you come under someone's scrutiny, show gratitude for that person's courage and perspective. If you are celebrating someone, humanize that person's results by focusing on the behavior that led to those extraordinary achievements. When providing feedback, rather than judging, maintain openness, seeking to understand how to move forward together. When people feel safe, they're naturally more productive. Instead of your team exerting energy directed at "CYA behaviors," provide a safe environment, so their efforts are focused on more constructive behaviors.

The fifth principle of Spartan Leadership is **Trustworthiness**. Creating a culture of trust and security allows teams to work together against the real obstacles that face them. Removing internal interference and promoting inclusion unites your team. When teams trust their leaders and the organization for which they work, accountability is a positive event as well as an equally-shared responsibility.

Chapter 6: Action Biased

For an organization to thrive, it must be able to adapt to its environment continually. The team must be able to identify then resolve issues and seize opportunity swiftly. Proficiency in 3 key actions is required.

The first is acting with limited information. You can always better prepare to understand a situation, but concepts are illusions until you take action. Key performance indicators (KPI's), are a common term used to describe the measured items that underpin the effectiveness of a group or process. Using KPI's allows you to make informed decisions with a limited amount of information. When it's clear where the opportunity lies and the means to make decisions is simple, the group can be more decisive. In almost any situation, there should be a single point of approval. Knowing the priorities and not creating procedural barriers primes those around you for action.

The second action is confronting fear. By understanding what information is essential, we can also determine the unknowns and our level of comfort in dealing with them. Within your comfort zone, there lies a boundary of decision paralysis – the point where you are uncomfortable moving in any direction. You can increase the distance that point is from the center of your comfort zone by developing your ability to improvise and act in the moment. Try new things that are unfamiliar and uncomfortable, to become better at improvising and living in the moment. Only when the leader shows how to deal with fear will those around him be able to navigate the unknown and act on faith.

external risks. In each example above, it is the leader's responsibility to provide security. When you come under someone's scrutiny, show gratitude for that person's courage and perspective. If you are celebrating someone, humanize that person's results by focusing on the behavior that led to those extraordinary achievements. When providing feedback, rather than judging, maintain openness, seeking to understand how to move forward together. When people feel safe, they're naturally more productive. Instead of your team exerting energy directed at "CYA behaviors," provide a safe environment, so their efforts are focused on more constructive behaviors.

The fifth principle of Spartan Leadership is **Trustworthiness**. Creating a culture of trust and security allows teams to work together against the real obstacles that face them. Removing internal interference and promoting inclusion unites your team. When teams trust their leaders and the organization for which they work, accountability is a positive event as well as an equally-shared responsibility.

Chapter 6: Action Biased

For an organization to thrive, it must be able to adapt to its environment continually. The team must be able to identify then resolve issues and seize opportunity swiftly. Proficiency in 3 key actions is required.

The first is acting with limited information. You can always better prepare to understand a situation, but concepts are illusions until you take action. Key performance indicators (KPI's), are a common term used to describe the measured items that underpin the effectiveness of a group or process. Using KPI's allows you to make informed decisions with a limited amount of information. When it's clear where the opportunity lies and the means to make decisions is simple, the group can be more decisive. In almost any situation, there should be a single point of approval. Knowing the priorities and not creating procedural barriers primes those around you for action.

The second action is confronting fear. By understanding what information is essential, we can also determine the unknowns and our level of comfort in dealing with them. Within your comfort zone, there lies a boundary of decision paralysis – the point where you are uncomfortable moving in any direction. You can increase the distance that point is from the center of your comfort zone by developing your ability to improvise and act in the moment. Try new things that are unfamiliar and uncomfortable, to become better at improvising and living in the moment. Only when the leader shows how to deal with fear will those around him be able to navigate the unknown and act on faith.

When it is easy to make decisions, and your team is fearless, curiosity is the final component of a call to action. Curiosity comes from ambition and a love of learning. Every person in the world is ambitious – without exception. Show me someone who is exhibiting "lazy" behaviors, and I'll show you someone who has motivations to exhibit that behavior. The key is not to attempt to change someone's ambition; it's to identify and amplify it. When you can effectively leverage that drive, people are receptive to intentional learning and development.

The sixth principle of Spartan Leadership is **Action Biased**. Our environment is everchanging. New obstacles and opportunities arise by the minute. For an organization to thrive, it must evolve more quickly than the challenges it faces. Encouraging the combination of simplicity, fearlessness, and curiosity on a team allows for action to take place. Action always generates one of two outcomes: experience-from which we learn, or progress toward the goals we set.

Chapter 7: Never Surrender

In Chapter 4, we left off with Lycurgus implementing his vision. Lycurgus realized that his plan was in place. The rebirth of Spartan culture was no longer an illusion, but a reality. He prepared himself to travel once again to the Oracle at Delphi for direction. He called the leaders of Sparta together to notify them of his intentions. He had each one swear an oath to uphold their new laws until his return. Little did they know they would not see their leader again.

When Lycurgus reached the Oracle, she offered him praise and confirmed that his vision would produce a great civilization. His name would live on throughout the ages. Lycurgus was satisfied with his accomplishments. Having bound the Spartans by oath to their new ways, his final act was one of sacrifice. Lycurgus never was seen again. Common belief holds that he starved himself, to never succumb to the temptation of returning home. This act ensured that his laws would last forever.

The result of Lycurgus's mission was the most dominant civilization in Greece's history. A widely-held belief at the time was that one Spartan soldier was worth many soldiers from any rival tribe. Spartan soldiers were the gold standard by which all others came to be measured. Sparta maintained a firm grip on southern Greece during this period by adhering to and improving upon the systems that were in place. The civilization thrived.

Lycurgus set the tone by showing he was willing to give his life for Sparta's future. His spirit lived on in the form of a Spartan's shield. A Spartan soldier viewed his shield with reverence. Not only did it represent his willingness to take up arms to protect his civilization, to become a part of the phalanx, but it was how he defended the lives of his fellow warriors. A Spartan soldier returned home after battle either with his shield or lying upon it. Spartans never surrendered, choosing death before dishonor.

The Spartans continued to be invincible for another 300 years, until they showed vulnerability in 425 B.C., surrendering to defeat. This display of submission caused their enemies to become more bold and aggressive. In 371 BC, Sparta suffered a significant loss to the Thebes army. After this, their allies abandoned them, leading to their final defeat. The civilization thrived until it lost its identity.

The seventh principle of Spartan Leadership is **Never Surrender**. The soul of your organization is its purpose. Maintain contact with it in every decision you make. When you achieve that purpose, consider how it can be best sustained. Can it be improved? The mission never truly ends. A legacy becomes established. The leader, the vision, and the purpose must be synonymous and in total harmony.

Conclusion

The story of Lycurgus and the Spartans of Ancient Greece serves as a powerful example of the influence an extraordinary leader can utilize to drive change. It is unlikely that Lycurgus could precisely map the path to achieving his final objective, or that he foresaw all the obstacles he would need to surmount along the way. Not having all the answers is acceptable. It's essential to note that when Lycurgus committed to the idea of restoring Sparta's culture, he began by developing *himself*. He invested time to travel extensively to discover the reforms that would perfect Spartan society. As Lycurgus grew, he embraced his newfound vision, and by utilizing his skills was able to gain the commitment of others, inspiring them to lead. He aligned his followers against the evils of his society, seized opportunities as they presented themselves, and ended his campaign by sustaining it. Spartan Leadership is a management approach tailored to guide a person through this growth process, from the early inception of a vision to its ultimate realization.

The leadership style contains seven principles to which you must adhere to achieve your vision. I've recapped these principals below:

Singular – The purpose of the organization is the point of origin for all actions.

People Focused – Those who follow you and those your organization serves are most important.

Accountable – Manage yourself before managing others. Develop self-awareness and lead by example to set the tone for your organization.

Rallying – Inspire others, both to increase your influence and to accelerate the rate at which your organization evolves.

Trustworthy – Promote security and trust, aligning your group against real obstacles.

Action Biased – Promote action and adaptation, remove encumbrances, and remain agile.

Never Surrender – Be authentic to your purpose, never betraying your founding principles.

The power and burden of leadership are incredible. As a leader, your responsibilities are almost infinite. They are also directly proportionate to your power and influence. The conclusion is straightforward: if you are willing to take responsibility for bringing your vision to life, through your journey, you will gain the power and influence necessary to succeed.

www.ingramcontent.com/pod-product-compliance
Lightning Source LLC
Chambersburg PA
CBHW072034230526
45468CB00021B/1804